The Sky is Not the Limit

and Other Select Poems

A Book of Poetry
by

R.T. Sedgwick

A Word with You Press®
Publishers and Purveyors of Fine Stories in the Digital Age
Moscow, Idaho

The Sky is Not the Limit: and Other Select Poems
is published by:
A Word with You Press®

310 East A Street, Suite B, Moscow, Idaho 83843

For information, please direct emails to:
info@awordwithyoupress.com or visit our website:
www.awordwithyoupress.com

Cover design and interior layout: Teri Rider, www.teririder.com
Cover art by Jim Sedgwick

Author's Limited Edition
Printed in the United States of America

10 9 8 7 6 5 4 3 2 1   15 16 17 18 19 20 21 22 23 24

Advance Praise for *The Sky is Not the Limit*

"R. T. Sedgwick's book, *The Sky is Not the Limit and other select poems*, offers the reader a feast of lively, sensual poems that are seeded with precise images and details as well as with a dash of sardonic humor. This book is a pleasure to read and savor."

> —Maria Mazziotti Gillan, *American Book Award Winner, and Professor of Poetry at Binghamton University, New York*

"This is a complete and well-formed collection. 121 poems. After years of crafting poetry with R. T., I thought I knew his measure as a poet, but this collection convinced me otherwise. His sure grip on colorful language and a wide diversity of subject matter makes this a very interesting read.

A poem-to-poem mixing of form in wild abandon. He has a sure grip of colorful language. R. T.'s quick mind and sure ear for the sound he intends to create are apparent throughout.

With his unrestrained imagination, R. T. was destined to be a poet. He sprinkles in form poems often enough to convince the reader of his mastery of them. And of shape, where thoughts seem to want to be a certain way on the page.

He takes a title like "Heads or Tails" and fills it with an unexpected verse.

He is not a poet of obscure words and phrases, the reader knows what R. T. is writing about.

This is a well rounded collection of his work. Its pacing will keep the reader interested with the mixture of form, style and substance. He has a large number of love poems. The male reader will find himself envious and exhausted.

This collection is one to be admired, both for its length and for its complexity."

> —Keith Van Vliet, *originator of The Valley Poets. 1983; Vice President of California State Poetry Society.*

for my five grandchildren
Beth
    Anna
        Calvin
            Will &
                Duncan
who have shown me that love
grows without bound
and even
    the sky is
        not the limit…

Contents

Foreword

Since my first book of poetry, *Left Unlatched*, which won the San Diego Book Award for best poetry book of 2011, I have continued to write poetry and be inspired by hundreds of poets—both local and world-wide, living and dead. Poetry has become a vital part of my life and it is a prime factor in helping me to live a grateful life filled with wonder and awe.

My writing centers around my home-office writing desk, my ever-growing shelves of poetry books and several local coffee houses. I attend two weekly workshops—Pleasures of Poetry—led by Harry Griswold in Solana Beach and—Poetry Overview Workshop—facilitated by Sandy Carpenter in Oceanside, as well as a monthly critique group that meets in the home of poet Kenneth Buhr in Poway. Most years I attend a weeklong summer poetry workshop at Idyllwild Arts in the beautiful San Jacinto Mountains. Other workshops I attend on a less-regular basis are, Raven Poets in Claremont and Valley Poets, which meets in Glendora at the home of Keith VanVliet. I have been published annually in the San Diego Poetry Annual, Magee Park Poets Anthology and the Ekphrastic Summations Anthology.

The title for this book, *The Sky is Not the Limit*, was inspired by an Ekphrastic poem of the same title, which appears as the last poem in the book. The artwork that inspired it was a computer creation by my son, Jim Sedgwick, titled "Primary Colors" and forms the basis for the book's cover. Both the artwork and companion poem were part of the annual art show at La Jolla Presbyterian Church. But *The Sky is Not the Limit* also clearly represents the breadth and depth as well as the height of the poems contained herein, ranging from birth to death and all of the mysteries and adventures in between.

The Sky is Not the Limit

and Other Select Poems

The Anchor I Needed

It was a doorknocker in the shape
of an anchor   a wedding present
somewhat cliché and useless for years
until we bought our own place

And so she brought it out of hiding
big smile on her face   still like new
packed in its white box with gold
Delta Gamma emblazoned on top

Handed it to me much the way
she did our first child
It seemed too heavy for its size
must be pure brass   I thought

Even as I screwed it to the front door
I wondered why we needed it
when we already had a door bell
She said everyone loves a door knocker

And she was my anchor till I lost her
It's been about a dozen years now
Sometimes I float along aimlessly
Still better than being in dry dock

I hadn't planned to stay out this late
so I didn't leave the porch light on
I fumble in the pitch of night
feeling for the keyhole

And as my key finally slips in
I raise the anchor once and let it fall
against its anvil   just for the sound
my *Anvil Chorus*   my welcome home

Songs of America

Music swim hard   swim fast
as you journey up the Mississippi
from the delta through New Orleans

to all points north bringing the blues
from cotton fields   choir lofts
juke joints   and lowly bordellos

songs of suffering sung by the poor
bring your guitars   your drums
your saxophones and harmonicas

bring Muddy Waters and B. B. King
the munificent ooh la la's of the blues
Oh music swim hard   swim fast

upstream to Natchez   Memphis
St. Louis and Cincinnati and soon
the entire country will be swooning

over the cornerstones of your songs
Chicago will swagger   Harlem will hop
gospel   Dixieland   ragtime   jazz

bluegrass   country   rock and roll
rhythm and blues   soul music   rap
the world will perk up its ears and bay

Oh music   swim hard   swim fast

Moon Musings

Look at me
        I am the moon
                I keep my distance
A lonely lover
        with nothing to be sad about
                for all I need is space
I tug at your oceans 24/7
        try to ignore the smoke
                and dust of your wars
Sometimes I feel
        like an empty dinner plate
                waiting to be filled
There's not a trace
        of a man in me as some of you
                Earthlings proclaim
I've heard you arguing
        whether I'm the size of a nickel
                dime or quarter
I know I seem brighter
        when you're on the back porch
                with your latest lover
And I'm sure you think I helped
        you fall in love again
                but that's pure illusion
I look at love like
        a handful of water
                or yesterday's snow
And one more thing
        keep that air of yours clean
                so I can get to you

Beach Glass

Evenings the desert turns pink
and multi-fingered Joshua trees
fuse into their own shadows

An eroded rock formation alludes
to *A Mighty Fortress Is Our God*
an ancient hymn of my childhood

when I searched junk piles and gutters
looking for colored glass to add glitter
to my sister's pretend jewelry store

which she no longer can remember
how she arranged them on cotton
spread out over several vanity mirrors

each with its own miniature price tag
smaller pieces always more expensive
like her brief smile of recognition today

Here the rippled dunes duplicate
themselves the way the sea repeats
in its assured and unrelenting way

and though it is miles from any ocean
I once picked up a scallop shell here
next to a sun-bleached cow-skull

Her life has turned partly pretend
by a disease I can't quite comprehend
yet facets of her still long to sparkle

Erosion in the desert can be harsh
like the pounding of breaking waves
so I keep a lookout for beach glass

Ode to the Pencil

O Pencillus   'little tail' in Latin
you wag through any language

your life span but a scribbled line
roughly 65 kilometers in length

deep within your painted shell
a million pent-up secrets tangle

always willing to fit snuggly
into smooth hand of poet or lover

yet never resisting the calloused
hand of accountant or kidnapper

sharp enough to make your point
yet no one ever asks for your opinion

what a humble drawn-out life you live
narrow pigment core of graphite

snug within a pod of painted wood
pink annihilator mounted on your back

as syllables cruise the length of paper
your useful life grows ever shorter

and in the end displaced by a clone
your epitaph a never burnt-out flame

We Need Words

Words to burrow through
those shimmering wrinkles
of hot dry air that lead us
like carrots dangling
from sticks   toward
the ever-receding oasis

Words to picture
brilliantly flared poppies
of Georgia O'Keeffe
words to hammer out
a Mendelssohn rondo
or evoke the haunting
of Mona Lisa's smile
the marbled maelstroms
of Michelangelo's David

Words for the light and
lack of light that greeted
Galileo when he first gazed
into his early telescope
words willing to propel
us over the precipice
not leave us hanging
in those unbalanced
pre-climax moments

Words to render tears
when death decides to swing
his ruthless scythe   words
to describe all the timeless
joy and sadness of existence
through which we trudge

Unpack the Trunk

look   at language   as   art
hear   it   as   music
touch   its   texture
savor its taste its aroma
free   each   element
from   semantic   obligation
and   don't   be   deceived
by   a   single   beautiful   word

Archeologist

Sifting through
sunken civilizations
of words   opening books
of ancient poetry
love in bits and pieces
saving shards
of fractured stoneware
spooning away
what we don't want
to see
plowing up the dirt
of dawn
sowing seeds of sadness
for another day

Trope-less in Seattle

A slow rain has been falling for hours
and I want to write a poem that wets
the page with pure unadulterated H_2O
so you'll get soaked when you read it

I don't want to use a single metaphor
so don't even think cats and dogs
nor is it raining like crazy or like hell
since I don't want any similes either

and forget images like red wheelbarrow
glazed in rainwater or faces that appear
as petals on a wet black bough   no
I am seeking the essence of wetness

I'd like to say water water everywhere
but it smacks too much of anaphora
and to say we're not wanting of water
would be downright assonance

This leads me to think that rain or maybe
nothing can be described in words without
the use of tropes so I guess I'll just sit back
and listen to the non-onomatopoeic rain

On Writing a Poem by the River

On a willow stump by the river I conger an image
of Li Po peering back at me from the other side

Not having to beg for an invitation   a breeze
envelops and enters through the pores of my skin

There's a fixed set of celestial laws prescribed
and I strive to follow the purveyor's intent

like one in a flotilla of bright yellow rowboats
submitting to some frivolous oarsman's whims

whose detailed manuscript of stars and planets
has never been signed   thus still anonymous

The moon paces the luminous overhead vault
like a ravenous woman with a reckless heart

My eyes follow the madness of her journey
and I wonder if she even notices their sadness

I pour another glass of wine and offer her a toast
It worked for Li Po so it will surely work for me

In Search of Raw Material

I walk aimlessly and watch the wind blow limbs
mostly bare   but for the budding nerve-ends of spring

I could be throwing stones at stars
or untying ribbons to unwrap the setting sun

no one would care   I deal mostly in second hand stuff
choose well when sifting through opulent rubble

and never take credit for a tree someone else planted
even though I may have pruned it with loving care

I traipse through trappings of tar hoping to find a feather
my moral code chiseled on a block of sea ice

The page holds its breath waiting for the next word
Oxygen comes   but only at the end of each line

and that can be faster than secrets passing through thin-
walled row-houses or slower than the hour hand of a clock

My intent is to enter the hungry mouth of emptiness
willing to be chewed up   swallowed and digested

and like a well-equipped spelunker work my way down
between jagged margins to the bottom of the page

First Draft

My father used to have a saying
You're not out of the woods yet
whenever he saw I was in trouble

I can almost hear his voice now
as I struggle to finish another poem
not even halfway out of the woods

surrounded by a thicket of stillness
oak   elm   hickory   pine
mired down on a rain-soaked road

all four wheels sunk deep in mud
trying to be like a stone that breathes
I inhabit this silence as though it were

my roof   my well   my nourishment
God surely must have felt the need
to look outward while first drafting

the universe   earth   man   woman
to speak of creation is to write a poem
and even He sees virtue in revision

Awash in Poetics

The ocean is writing poetry again
coining the words it needs
to express power   beauty   love
vowels loosely tossed
in the foam of breaking waves
soprano a's   e's   i's
harmonizing with their softer altos
and a baseline of o's & u's
curling them down to smash
into consonants with dissonance
skroo-wosh   zis-krooz   skroo-wosh
then a bubbling ebb of froth and foam
pipps   zizzes   iffs & *ollas*
repeated refrains like broken
pantoums or villanelles
and from its depths the dolphins
mate to oboe melodies
as orcas serenade while oysters
simply lie in silence making pearls
overhead   gulls and pelicans
rejoice with poons   koots   mulus
most of the earth's surface immersed
in the fluent alphabet of the sea

#2 Dixon Ticonderoga

Don't let the high-gloss yellow skin
mislead you   I am not a cowardly lion

I've been known to take on the sword
scribble out manifestos   conquer empires

dash out letters   wills   and epitaphs
but like you I too have my daily routines

composing grocery lists   keeping golf
or bridge scores   filling out long forms

maybe a note or two to stick on the fridge
lots of crossing out   editing   erasing

And my life-style's a lot like yours as well
I prefer being sharp rather than dull or broken

I worry a little about my ever-eroding eraser
and my shortness   I'm turning into a stub

It's that infinite store of unwritten possibilities
in my center core that continues to inspire me

It's as though some inner voice keeps saying
You are the muse that links poet to page

The Thick Scalding Sweetness of Love

What happens between us
has happened for centuries

bright as glass   inexhaustible
and true   All the new thinking

is about loss   like sitting dry
atop a pile of ancient sawdust

a moment and it is gone
But we are made more beautiful

by losses   Our eyes can see
what our hands do   yet they do it

because it feels real   like the yellow
of bananas   hence we go to such

furnishings   swing open the door
on nothing but blue smoke   Outside

burly old fruit trees in mist and rain
rejoice in their own ecstasies

You've Found the Perfect Woman

but then one fine day you learn
that she too has a skeleton
hanging in the back of her closet

you had suspected it all along
but this woman   so lovely in her bones
one wouldn't think she'd need an extra set

then one night   maybe you were a bit blunt
but you said   I'll show you mine
if you'll show me yours   and so

you take her by the hand and open
your closet door   push aside the shirts
but your skeleton is nowhere in sight

at her place   she opens up her closet
sweeps apart the dress-laden hangers
no bones lurking in there either

then you hear a slight noise like the creak
of a bedspring so you both turn around
to find your skeletons madly clanking away

you look at one another and laugh
begin unbuttoning each other's clothes
lust   it's been thriving in your bones

The Night-birds

I want to pluck you like a plum
swallow your flesh
and savor the pit
to be planted later
peel you from the sticker book
and paste you into my poem

for we are like two sides
of a right triangle
with love our hypotenuse
striding in on the steed of spring
and it's always spring when I sleep
next to your dark brown hair

the ghost of desire follows me
like a fading rocket plume
but you know how to shorten the time-lag
between wanting and getting
for you are the breaking wave
and I the shore

you move ever so slowly
into this midnight madness
roll me up and twist
my ends like a tootsie roll
then tug at me till I come
unwrapped   even now

I can almost smell the yeast
as the end of night-shift nears
and I think of you taking off
your little baker's apron
folding and tucking it under your arm
walking the few blocks back
to where the crows perch

on poles projecting from our
pink-painted casita where we
begin with breathing exercises
until we become one
permanently fastened
and the night-birds burst into flame

Where We Touch

It's been said that creation began
with the separation of light
from darkness and that light is good
and although not stated
one might infer that darkness
is not so good but maybe it's the fear
of darkness that's bad   a wolf
in the shadows beyond our porch light
for even the distant stars are surrounded
by darkness   like golden raisins
imbedded in a bran muffin   so surely
light and darkness have a longing
to rejoin   a strong attraction
to intermingle forever   we might call it
a magnetism or maybe even a desire
love being the boundary
where the two touch   and since you
are the light of my world   I'm dying
to be the wild darkness surrounding you

Witness Protection

Was it the necklace
or the double-stranded pearls
of the necklace   or maybe

the silver thread that held
(then didn't hold) them together
around her slender neck

Or was it how they curved
toward her delicate breasts
as she removed her blouse

Or how she pursed her lips
as she asked me to unclasp it
my fingers turning all thumbs

so we forgot it altogether
until the silver thread broke
and the pearls spilled out

later we laughed together
as we plucked them from
the sheets and cold linoleum

put them in a draw-string bag
in her jewelry box   protector
of witness to our little crime

These Words

The universe was content
articulating itself
in lights and shadows
no words needed
grains of sand were
never defined nor
compiled into dictionaries
then the human race
exerted its presence
with simple gestures
turning chatter into words
that we might let our hearts
speak of their desires
their fantasies
so when you read the note
I left on your nightstand
as you were sleeping
know that these words
are from the very core
of my being
lay them down beside you
read them over and over
sew them into the hem
of your pillowcase

Wild Dewberries

It was late summer and we knew wild
dewberries would be primed for picking

You handed me a tattered Easter basket
resurrected from some long-ago egg hunt

where you found the coveted black egg
with numeral thirteen inscribed in yellow

It meant you had won the grand prize
a free ticket to Baptist Summer Camp

where among other things you unearthed
the ecstasies of wild dewberry hunts

The counselors knew nothing of how you
seduced boys with your lucky basket

I smiled at your little story and took your
hand as we headed toward Becker's Hill

past the pond where the willow tree bends
low and stirs the water with its branches

as though writing rambling love letters
in a longhand both of us could understand

We could almost smell the uncertainty and yet
wanted to be in a state of longing for nothing

The dewberries stained your lips and I could
taste their sultry sweetness on your tongue

In the light of afternoon we viewed the world
like the sweet mystery that swelled from within

as we traced uncharted landscapes of our wild
and filled your lucky basket to the brim

The Power of Love

I could never walk past love
ignore it completely
the way I sometimes do hunger

For without it I am only a void
in the surrounding air
that takes the shape of my body

I remember our first slow dance
a bit awkward at first   until
we became a single moving shape

Oh how I wish love were simply
some ripe fruit that we could share
bite by succulent bite

The way splashing ocean waves
explain themselves over and over
and then again   to the shores

Had we been born grains of sand
I'd need love to conquer any wave
keeping me   from reaching you

The Immortality of Love

though we never set out to prove it
you and I have died in each other's arms

> and more than a million times over
> swimming the strands of your dark brown hair

> > scaling the cliffs of my rocky tor
> > not wanting to prove anything

other than to stay alive long enough
to die one more beautiful death

> so when white water begins to rage
> and the rubber raft self-inflates

> > we secure the ropes around our waists
> > ready our pitons   and yes

we swim and we climb

The Colonnade

Today the air smells a bit mischievous
 as the wind wraps its muscular arms
around a cluster of riveting thunderheads
squeezing out sparks of rain   Come I say
and we duck into the crowded colonnade
A tiny lizard   eyes deeper than any question
either of us could ask and quicker than
the zigzag footwork of lightning tapping
out its celestial dance   catches our attention
He scurries up the shaft of one of the fluted
Doric columns diverting our wonderment
from the narrow slits of worsening skies
between them   How quickly daylight trips
over darkness   You take my hand   We melt
into last night's shower scene as the crowd
fades and your arms drape over my shoulders
mine both bound to your waist   The river
below with its oxbows and suspended bridges
flows so freely we suspect it must have left
its secrets back in the mountains the way
vines in sunlight seem free of their roots'
dark strivings or the way last week's kisses
float only in memory   The sea in the distance
is a sermon in salt and silence where sound
waves are laid to rest like unspoken prayers
we never even knew we were praying

The Art of Making Curry

How easily happiness
can sometimes
get a kick-start
from a single tap
on the bottom
of a curry powder can
sending monsoons
of toasty-gold dust
onto a hot skillet
as she stirs the oil
with a wooden spoon
I from behind
arms wrapped tightly
about an aproned waist
am her crazy lover
doing the tapping
and we fit
our bodies fit
we fit all over
she adds chopped onions
the steam ascends
transports us
into a state of frenzy
we turn down the stove
and slip to the floor
like two cobras
after flute music ends
and our lips fit
our souls fit
we have found Nirvana

Summer Love

Drops of warm late-summer rain
      play out a syncopated rhythm
            on the tin roof of the barn

Purple Prairie seed bags
      make perfect pillows side by side
            in the dimly lit hayloft

Dry straw from a broken bale
      of new-born-animal bedding
            becomes our makeshift mattress

First time for the two of us
      ducked in here as refugees
            of a sudden summer shower

Fruit we'd gathered
      from apricot and plum trees
            adds a still-life composition

On a broad plank of the hayloft floor
      I carve a simple heart
            surrounding our initials

Rain that started with a pitter-patter
      picks up its rhythmic pace
            and taking cue   we follow

Cementing memories that will bring us back
      to these lofty heights long after
            the rains of that long-ago summer

Snowbound

Notes of Chopin flutter
through the clutter of our little
room like snowflakes beyond
the windowsill swelling drifts
into loaves of unbaked bread

Remember when you said
*My God we are quite the unlikely
item* and I replied *Upon first pairing
many things seem odd*

Tonight we'll huddle
like two half-notes slurred
in the sagging center of our bed
and you'll request Revel's Bolero
while all around us snowplows
clear the streets for morning

Rules for Making Love

A man goes far to find out what he is
or what he wants out of life   I once
wrote a little book of rules for making love
I made my bed the imaginary resting place
for preface and introduction   I thanked
anyone in advance who might offer me
real-life suggestions   I disguised myself
as a man-on-the-street radio announcer
taking an opinion poll   A guy rummaging
through a dumpster told me to never give up
on anything   A young librarian claimed love
was like still waters echoing the mood of sky
and the UPS Man said it is better to deliver
than to receive   I never know what to do
with my hands and I can feel the darkness
even when it's light   I seem stranded
I suffer when a bird hits the window
Not even I can outrun anguish   That heart
left on the pillow must be either yours
or mine   At last the pearly dawn arrives
and I am able to count each breath again

Scented but Unsent

Even before I met you I could feel
the curves of your hips in my hands

The air in that room became as inviting
as a late crop of pure lavender lilacs

and light lingered there like long
summer mornings of childhood

In our time both love and war will come
and go   but today I write of love

I long to live in that part of you
that is unfamiliar even to yourself

that place that made you quiver
the first time you heard your mother cry

I will always be thinking about the mystery
of that gravitational pull between us

As spring goes quickly skipping by we find
ourselves suddenly deep inside of autumn

We listen to Charlie Parker or rock 'n' roll
but then switch to Mozart to feel moved

Simple pleasures like a cup of black coffee
brisk walks in the park or even the orgasms

we share are insufficient to define our oneness
but there are laws on this planet we must live by

As I type this letter to you in my little rectangle
of light so many people outside of it are dying

When old beginnings pass us by
we must forge on to find new ones

Ripe with Love

I want to be that top banana
plucked from a stately bunch
of yellows gently peeled by you

I want to be that red bandana
tucked neatly around our picnic lunch
with a flask of Merlot and a toast to you

I want to be that golden lantana
that showy bouquet I got on a hunch
it would signal the longings I have for you

I want to be the man in your cabana where
hours turn to minutes like time being crunched
as we handle the furnishings   just me and you

Newlyweds

It was the sixties
I bought you that paper dress
the only one you ever owned

Pop-art pink flowers
on a green background
from Waste Basket Boutique

You didn't like it
but you wore it anyway—
to the Happening

Not a lot happened
some loud music and beer
a few rips in that dress

When we got home
you dared me to tear it off
and here   the story begins

Return to Sender

I wrote you this rambling love letter last week
as October's downed leaves were blowing

chasing the final iotas of Summer's sweetness
from dwindling fruit to fermenting wine

The day's shadows on the backyard sundial
had pulled hard at time's axis all afternoon

and the solitary swan down on Green Pond
seemed nothing more than a cardboard cut-out

In the misted distance I remember hearing
muted echoes of a man calling his lost dog

The gray procession of days had brought back
moonlight that once bathed your ash-blond hair

I can't see myself ever re-reading this letter
and so I'm shredding it into mulch for the roses

Above the trees dark wings lift on a curved
path as migration once again heads south

Making Hay

Such power
        came down
                from the clouds
that afternoon   hay making stopped

Cool drops
        of sweet rain
                splashed our faces
as hired hands ran to the barn for cover

Still in the field
        Alta and I removed
                each other's clothes
and settled into the fresh-cut clover

For a short time
        our world had shrunk
                to her lips and mine
clinging through the final cloudburst

Was it the rain
        our craziness   or love
                who knows
it's all tangled up in a bale of memories

Love

He never understood
the full meaning of the word
but knew if he ever uttered it
in one of his weak moments
in the presence of any
of those loose chicks
who after long rounds of drinking
went riding with him on the back
of his Harley and ended up
in some deserted lane
it was tantamount to signing
a long term lease on his penis
and that's why when he first heard
the word in the men's recovery group
the tattooed tiger on his right bicep
almost leapt off his skin
and the gold ring dangling
from his earlobe shuddered
so later when I hugged him I slipped
the word in with a warning
I am about to say the 'L-word'
but that was last year and today
when you see him wrap his tattooed
arms around one of the new guys
you know he's found the meaning
of the word even if you can't hear
his low whisper   *Love ya man*

Love Was Our Savior

Wrought in the furnace of some distant galaxy
I entered this world through its front door
soon to find there is also one marked exit
Other doors are for use only in case of fire

You begged me to trim your courtyard hedge
Soon we became an island in a sea of grass
living out our lives like loose change in a purse
Art and poetry became mirrors of our dreams

As affections altered us logic was spaded under
We broke the vase on which our verse was written
Marriage can be a push-each-other's-button world
We vowed not to let novelty stray from its leash

As seasons spiraled we re-worked the garden
leaving room for love to cavort like children
kept our distance from the doors marked fire
watched night dance down the hazy purple hills

Love on a Flagpole
—after Poem About People
by Robert Pinsky

When I read poems composed
by other poets I'm always inspired
For example I wouldn't have thought
of running love up a flagpole if not
for the line *But how love falters*
and flags in a Robert Pinsky poem

So I made a simple one of white satin
with two overlapping hearts in pink
and red and it's been out on my pole
for all to enjoy but with barely no wind
or breeze it just hangs like a limp rag
so no one ever sees its drooping hearts

That was until yesterday when you came
by for a cup of coffee and a stiff wind
caused the flag to inflate its pink and red
Later when we switched to Chardonnay
and the touch of fingertips turned electric
love fluttered like no flag ever before

Imprint

There was a woman I made love to
and how I remember the setting

the curved path wending its way down
to where it leveled off at the river's edge

the tall reeds that sheltered us from view
of anyone passing along the main trail

the hesitancy of the dragonfly to land
the occasional splash of jumping fish

perfume of peppermint and clover rising
from the crushed foliage beneath us

and afterward the sound of birdsong
emanating from the tops of sycamores

their thinning branches stretching skyward
reaching for strewn wisps of cirrus clouds

this woman who read me like a book
and who left its pages carelessly open

Hot Bath

Sometimes a hot bath
is just a hot bath
sometimes it's an orgy
involving a guest list
as varied as the bar scene
in Star Wars and other times
it's just the two of us
gently slathering soapsuds
over different body parts
with terrycloth mitts
repeating a stroke whenever
we hear that barely audible
sigh   for we both know
that cleanliness
is next to godliness
you Calliope   me Apollo
and afterwards we can be
any god or goddess we choose
as we rinse off each others'
cares of the day
and towel down
into a long night's sleep
in anticipation
of Olympian dreams

Deep in the Woods

Desire was everywhere and it spoke
      louder than the woodland violets
          louder than the whip-poor-wills

The gray sky hung on like an endless goodbye
      tugging at daylight's monolithic drive
         to go on no matter what

Everywhere we could feel the fingerprints
      of the gods   In the distance the slurred
        half-notes of a raven

We fashioned a pallet out of fallen leaves
      began unbuttoning our decorum
         wanting to blend into the wild

The wind from the river pulsed against your face
      and you held mine together
         as though it were a broken mask

We understood how the woods might
      feel the emptiness of a single fallen tree
         so we vowed we'd stay together

Knowing now why Eve offered Adam
      a taste of that forbidden fruit
         and why he accepted

Bodies in Motion

the space-time frame of a king-size bed
dips and swirls as two bodies

orbit each other like binary stars
until their crystalline flutes shatter

and rivers of champagne slowly seep
into the depths of each other's sleep

and they barely notice their foreplay
as the following night begins with a toast

using reconstructed champagne glasses
filled with an even bubblier vintage

rekindling splendors of the past
that will stretch out before them

Blackberries

—after Don McLean
lyrics to Vincent

We came to pick blackberries
on the far hill through golden wheat
and cornflower bloom as though
walking into a Van Gogh painting
bringing these lyrics to life
> *Blissful summer day*
> *paint the sky in blue and gold*
> *wistful hues that won't grow old*
> *nor fade the vibrant saffron of your hair*
> *passion never dies*
> *flash those black-eyed-susan eyes*
> *catch hold of love before it flies*
> *and tuck it in the hillside of your heart*

We fill our wicker basket and then
on a blanket near patches of silkweed
that sprout through a barbed wire fence
lay in communion with nature's gifts
in the summer sun of the hillside
and feast on plump sweet berries

Proposal Letter Pantoum

Let's jump right into the heart of this letter
put the core ahead of the apple   I guess
it's seeds not flesh that make this world better
to some that seems backwards   I must confess

Put the core ahead of the apple   I guess
yet always keeping our future in mind
to some that seems backwards   I must confess
we've got nothing to lose but a lot to find

Yet always keeping our future in mind
knowing we'll chase the American Dream
we've got nothing to lose but a lot to find
now that we're back on track as a team

Knowing we'll chase the American Dream
two kids and a dog and a white picket fence
now that we're back on track as a team
give me a kiss   it'll end the suspense

Two kids and a dog and a white picket fence
a big front yard and a garden with flowers
Give me a kiss   it'll end the suspense
as soon as we marry   the dream will be ours

A big front yard and a garden with flowers
It's seeds not flesh that make this world better
as soon as we marry   the dream will be ours
Let's jump right into the heart of this letter

As We Make Love

the world grows quieter
and the war around us
ceases

as though we are deep
in a sound-proof
bunker

sensing the myriad
of places our bodies touch
your breath   mine

but love cannot hide
from war forever   too soon
we'll be expelled

back onto the battlefield
like bees
buzzing from rose to lily

trying to avoid
the next higher link
in the food chain

how painful it is to watch
flowers succumb
to trucks and tanks

flattened by boots
the dignity of their petals
stripped

by the blast of another
mortar shell
and so we must come

together again
for the world grows quieter
as we make love

Toast to Bride and Groom

So different
though moonlight paints
you as one

So attractive
like opposite poles
of a magnet

So complete
the final two brushstrokes
of a classic painting

So similar
like a pair of fleece-lined
bedroom slippers

So refreshing
a waterfall cascading
into a mountain lake

So inspiring
two crystalline bells
echoing into the future

Bow Wave

washed up
      on the shore
            of an unknown
                world
                    by waves
from a storm that began the night before
after too much wine   a spat   omen of albatross
but urgings to re-kindle by a pallid moon
                 turned us
          around
        and brought us
     reeling back
to good ground

Unspooling River

With evening's blue wash hung on a line
stretched from here to where the western sky
bends down to kiss that distinct protrusion
of earth we've nicknamed Becker's Hill
darkness takes on myriad dynamic shapes
kicking pant legs   flailing arms of shirts
sheets that remember last night's shimmy

I feel myself being siphoned into a past
that is itself an endless unspooling river
reaching beyond Emerson's Pond so tranquil
yet with ripples   cattails swaying
to the silent breath of wind

In this dream I never *exactly* dreamed I am lonely
as a child's kite caught in the walnut tree
above a young mother's clothesline
there's music   reeds   strings   woodwinds
all kindle for a fire focused at the end of a cane-pole
that my grandfather is brandishing like a giant torch
to wipe out the year's crop of walnut worms

The last hope of summer has long since dwindled
into autumn and the green canopy of Brock's Woods
has turned gold and bronze as time fades
for each and every unnamed leaf
the ones in the walnut tree having left weeks ago

I watch this on-going tug-o'-war between form and time
knowing that form is the one that must eventually lose
earth   air   fire   water   symphony of sound
with a crescendo that shakes me from my sleep
and a new slant of light spills through the blinds

Ode to Spring Rain

This morning the world
      was occupied with growing
Everywhere
      a perplexity
            of freshness
that wasted no time
      waiting for someone like me
stretched out
      on my patio
            chaise lounge
but it's evening now
      and I'm back out sweeping
my flashlight
      over all the bursting
            forth
till I spot a single firefly
      illuminating a lilac flower
I stand in awe
      as I too grow
            in realization
that nothing is needed of me
      other than thanks to a chilled
breeze for picking
      the locks
            of the clouds
that somehow know
      the real beauty
is in the growing
      as it frees
            its pent-up rain
The tall tulips know as they bow
      to their weight and the creek
knows as it gurgles
      louder
            and louder

Town's people sleep
       as flowers keep opening
and stars wide awake
       but hidden by clouds
            can't watch the ivy
slowly creeping up fences
       but the life-giving grace
of unlocked rain
       continues to fall
            continues to bless

The All-forgiving Sea

Another Monday morning and that sea
within sinks into a deep blue meditation

My face lists like a ship taking on water
as I try to scrape debris from life's deck

A familiar blue-violet haze descends
to smooth over last weekend's rubble

I clamber up the long rope of reason
only to peer at life through smoked-glass

The truth is I'm settling toward the bottom
like a tired jelly fish with worn-out tentacles

But the afternoon light always redeems me
just by emphasizing the outline of my being

So I reset my sails for yet another voyage
knowing the all-forgiving sea will prevail

The Winged Fisher

All morning long I monitor
the great blue heron
elbow deep in lagoon-water
soaking in his existence
and all I can think of
is I can't take this with me
not to the grave
nor even into the future
for memory has a way
of reaching back
only for the bits and pieces
images burned deep
into gray matter
like lavender body feathers
paired black head-plumes
S-shaped neck

The mullet fish are jumping
and soon one is within reach
of his long beak which opens
like barbecue tongs
to clamp its unsuspecting prey
and swallow it whole
I think to myself surely
I will take this at least
to the edge of my grave
if not even farther
as the heron spreads
a six-foot wingspan
and like an angel glides off
into his own blue heaven

Pantoum of Winters Past

On winter nights when snow came down
and we lay snuggly tucked in bed
hills turned white around the town
awoke the wooden homemade sled

while we lay snuggly tucked in bed
till dawn unrolled sun's ball of yarn
awoke the wooden homemade sled
across the street in Milnor's barn

when dawn unrolled sun's ball of yarn
like playful kittens out we'd go
across the street to Milnor's barn
steeped in splendor brought by snow

like playful kittens out we'd go
pulling the sled by its knotted rope
steeped in splendor brought by snow
that filled the woods and glazed the slope

cloud cover softened the blinding haze
as hills turned white around the town
forged memories for later days
on winter nights when snow came down

Music of the Rain

Rain trickles
note by bent-note
in cycles
of jazz and blues
keeping close
to the surface
of all things
like brushes
sliding rhythmically
over stretched
rawhide
of snare drum
simple showers
bringing nourishment
to weeds
and flowers alike
and who are we
to judge
which is which

As a child
my favorite flower
was the lowly
dandelion
I was attracted
to poorly kept lawns
un-cut
and weedy-yellow
and I loved the rain
not just for its music
but for its indiscrimination

Love Poem with Lilacs and Sycamore

We wake up as strangers to the rest of our lives
knowing that hope can fade like a mid-day moon
so touch me where no one else has touched me

Today is another opening of an imaginary door
and before its closing we need points of focus—
iris   nape of the neck   curvature of breast

We are flotsam in the whitewater of a twisty river
and we learned early on in arithmetic that anything
left over must be carried like so much bilge water

It's so easy to think lilacs once you've seen them
the world pulsates in a rotation of endless desire
look how the gnarly apple tree celebrates spring

I am certain that lovers have passed this way before
for longing whirls through nights like Van Gogh stars
poetry must be our daily devotion to unpredictability

the high road to achieving all that we've longed for
Outside our window a leaf falls from the sycamore
signaling that somewhere another bud is forming

Life Cycle

Slow down and tend the lines
of this poem as though a tomato

patch you've been invited to enter
by a close   perhaps best friend

notice the marks of the hand cultivator
how no weed has been left in its wake

commune with the yellow blossoms
the small green orbs that in summer

will awaken to the sun's fiery rays
come to life and burn with a redness

that you will cherish as you slice them
in your kitchen for an evening meal

then come back to the garden at the end
of summer and note the tangled lifeless

vines   restless for being dead as though
they still remember the joy in giving

It's Fall

when thoughts turn
to that split second
between summer's goodbye
and winter's hard hello

stalls of flowers
and fruit abound
the sky ahead
opaquely bright

breath spirals upward
like smoke
veined leaves vie
in fiery competition

then descend
like broken wings
a litter of questions
on the forest floor

carved hearts on birches
wait patiently for spring
to give the trees her gift
of green again

The Child Within
*—Our children teach us what life
is all about.* -Angela Schwindt

I keep
that little boy
I was
in my pocket
for childish situations
when I want to foot-stomp
       He comes in
       handy

Sometimes
I think I'd like to
quash him
but I could never do that
for he's the rainforest
of my poet-brain
       Sole supporter
       of an entire eco-system

Blake's tiger
Carroll's Jubjub bird
Tate's ape
a living menagerie
of image and metaphor
       If destroyed
       darkness remains

Summer's Over

You remember the days
when summers meant vacation
and you thought they'd never end

each morning the same swing
two twisted ropes and notched board seat
hanging from the same black walnut tree

each morning the same pair of robins
playing hop-scotch in front of the white lilac bush
singing   *male-and-tillie   male-and-tillie*

and always the same aroma
of griddle cakes and coffee escaping
through the rusted kitchen screen door

then as the sun inched higher overhead
lawn mowers came alive and outboard motors
from the distant lake buzzed like honeybees

and before you knew it summer was over—
it must be like that for my newly 4-year-old grandson
today at the party he said   *Pappy   you are old*

as he rubbed the back of a hand I barely recognize
but even before I could pull together a response
he was off to the swing his father had just put up for him

Smell the Hollyhocks

Papa told me
to smell the hollyhocks
that I'd always find one
blooming at nose level

and so I stood entranced
out on the east side
of the Red House
where the hollyhocks grew

I was three   then four
then five   and he was right
I always found a hollyhock
in bloom at nose level

saw the narrow
clapboard siding
turn to gray
as its red paint peeled

I have since grown
older and taller
than the hollyhocks
but they are gone now

like Papa
and the Red House
but I still remember
to seek nose-level blooms

catch nose-level scents
that come with the wind
run with them   smell them
like hollyhocks

Prodigal's Lament

His nightly escapades
of late have led
to the same painful
dénouement
Slumped body found
in unshaven heap
He prayed and knew
help would come
but was surprised to see it
in the form of a cloud
with razor in hand
following him
from Nick's saloon
to the back room
of a seedy bar
to Tilly's Whorehouse
scraping at whiskers
like a father
towering over
a young son
lather on his face
razor stroking
hair slicked back saying
time to clean up
and come to the table

Out of Body

I keep my memories neatly packed
in unmarked suitcases and old trunks
stacked in dark corners of boxcars
kites   cats   crow's feet   organ
grinders   sidetracked somewhere
between Tinsel Town and Timbuktu

I unpack them at the strangest of times
Ribbons   bon fires   pine trees   painted
lips   like today curled up in my window seat
staring at the ridges on my thumbnail that run
from clipped edge back to that little moon
like rippled ice on Emerson's Pond and

now I'm skating its frozen corrugated surface
tight black turtle neck   plaid scarf flapping
cutting sleek figure eights over bumpy ice
willy-nilly seducing my latest sweetheart
I swear I do this so well it feels real

Green Walnuts

How do I describe it
that pungent aroma contrived
by the green walnut

Not exactly moonshine
mingled with lemon peel
nor vodka with honey added

But its smell can be intoxicating
and as a boy I remember picking them
from the big tree in our front yard

Holding them up to my mother's nose
and waiting for her to inhale
followed by a sound I assumed

in later years to be not unlike
a sigh she may have uttered at climax
as she and my father made love

So don't be astonished the next time I
describe the smell of a fresh green walnut
as that of a mother's transcendent smile

Fish Ain't Bitin'

here I sit again
fishing for the moon
of youth

feet dangling
off the end of a pier
of many planks

dragonflied bobber dancing
across its laughing
reflection

Evensong

It's Good Friday again and my sister Sally and I
spend most of the morning cutting up seed potatoes
making sure we leave at least one eye in each chunk

then coat them with a smelly yellowish fertilizer
heavy in sulfates   filling more than five gunny sacks
which we load into the back of our pickup truck

We sing *Old MacDonald Had A Farm* as our father
drives us to the rented field out past the edge of town
next to *The Sisters of the Precious Blood* convent

We plant them all by hand   one potato chunk per hill
and always on Good Friday when the moon is just right
so the new potatoes will be ready by the 4th of July

As shadows of dusk lengthen we rush to finish our work
then pause as flute music from a lone Nun in the hills
reminds us what it was that made *this* Friday so good

Eddies

This morning I've allowed meaningless eddies of gray matter
        to morph into whirlpools of fear   journeying
                across the magic carpet of my five-year-old mind
like whirling Dervishes or twisters crossing a Kansas landscape
        as I sit cross-legged in Aunt Lucille's leaky rowboat
                bailing water with a #1 Campbell soup can

My cousin Tony's slim body   poised and confident
        stands like a statue on the cantilevered diving board
                at the end of Kimmel's pier
waiting until we are out beyond the drop-off
        before diving in and swimming out to join us
                showing me what a good swimmer he is

I can't swim that far or fast yet   so I try to focus
        on the small eddies that spin away from the dipping oars
                each time Aunt Lucille takes another stroke
My heart quickens as Tony bounces once then arches into the air
        disappearing beneath a shiny splash then surfacing
                in a perfect Olympic-style front crawl

The eddies in my mind say maybe he won't make it this time
        and we'll have to go back and pick him up
                but he always reaches us and receives his praise
I just keep bailing and hope the boat doesn't sink as my eddies
        slowly switch to thoughts of Aunt Lucille and Mom's
                life-saving sugar cookies once we reach the shore

Charged

I was sketching my idea
of a Picasso on the blackboard
using the one piece of chalk
in the fifth-grade classroom

You didn't like the way I drew
the intertwined hearts
so I handed the chalk to you
and our fingers touched

Electricity generated years ago
still lights my fingertips today

Barn Dance

It was during the hard-to-hide-desire period
of my youth that I hung out at the dance hall
on Saturday nights where tension at times
could rise to that of a snapped fiddle string

She was the youngest and best-of-the-breed
of three sisters who was always there to flirt
and dance and be taken home by somebody
so my ego kicked in when I was the lucky guy

The barn door was always open   a black hole
in a moonlit picture   nothing in front of it
nothing behind   till we crossed the threshold
lights out   crickets chirping all around us

She had learned the routine from her sisters
to let the night air   the scent of clover hay
the moonlight filtering through the rafters
feed us   the only two animals in the barn

Remembrance

This morning I noticed frost
on the jack-o'-lantern
just outside my front door
and began to wonder if anything
in nature might lead me to a place
as familiar as the paint-flaked
window sill where Grandma
cooled her pumpkin pies

I'm surrounded by sights
that strike sparks in such fancy
A passing face that takes me back
to a long-ago prom date whose name
hangs on the tip of my tongue
like a child not wanting to reveal
some long-hidden secret

Drawing water from memory's well
can at times joggle me for days
over miles of cobblestone streets
but sometimes the ride is smoother
like tonight as I touch the yellow
ribbon you tied so meticulously
around the tulips you sent me
evoking those many ritual nights
of removing
        your Tea-house
           silk pajamas

Wild Time

This morning I decided to ask Time if she would stop
and talk with me   *I can't stop*   she said
but you're welcome to walk along beside me

I rarely give interviews or empty my thoughts like this
but I'm tired of the way people talk about me
having me   not having me   taking me   spending me

and it really hurts when they think they are wasting me
Everybody says they tell me   and eventually I will tell
but they aren't telling me a damn thing nor will I ever tell

People say I hang heavy   or I'm a healer of all things
They invest in me   race against me   and have me to kill
Sometimes they stall for me   or run out of me

Prisoners say they are serving time   or doing time
and I frequently hear that I stop   or fly
Probably the closest any one comes is when they say I march on

But even that's not quite right   it's more like a prowl
As much as people think they know me   no one really does
What they experience is my trusty lion and his smashing paws

The Artistry of Tattletale

Tattletale tattletale hanging on a bull's tail
When the bull has to pee you will get a cup of tea
—Simon J. Bronner: American Children's Folklore

We learn early that nobody likes a tattletale

Little Mary who monitors every minute
on the playground at recess

reports each jot and tittle of misbehavior
earns the title of *Teacher's Pet*

The dull gray look of white linen haunting souls
who won't buy Proctor & Gamble's bleach

Lipstick on a collar that leads straight to divorce court
or the confidant who exposes a sex scandal

Somewhere in a moonlit desert a spy exposes
his position as he laser-paints an enemy asset

hoping in that vulnerable moment an armed drone
will kill his target before he is annihilated

But tattletale is an art so the whistle blower will keep
on blowing then simply shrug off the consequences

the way a tough shrub shivers in the cold wind

The Alarm Clock Expounds

I sometimes think you're jealous
of the space I take among perfumes
on your tiny dressing table

I see my face reflected daily
in the dark of your eyes
as you fuss and gussy up to go

Each of your momentary glances
is an eternity for me
between tick and tock

I know I represent conflict for you
since I keep constant track
of your over-scheduled life

You wind me with faith each night
and sometimes forget to set
my alarm   but don't blame me

for I can only see   and know
where my hands have been
and where yours have not

Sleep Interrupted

Night comes again in her negligee
to read me like an open book

never sure of where she left off
the previous night   no bookmarks

skipping everything that happened today
paging further and further into the future

I am like an unending farce and always
with more doors than can be opened

in one reading   giant black birds
fly in through the ones that are ajar

darting about the room in jealous rage
their wing-spines bat-like and threatening

causing shadows to move down my page
even at 3:00 a.m. she slams the book shut

leaving me wide awake and wondering
why the reading stopped dead in its tracks

Roughing It Out

I paint the rip-roaring red flags
      green

comb the tangles out of groggy
      language

clutter in my house is the clutter
      of a mind

always another door to open
      another empty room to fill

I don't intervene in the duel between
      smiles and tears

another birthday   I blow out
      the candles   inchworm on

thoughts of you roll over in my bed
      I let them roll

Portfolio Blues

The market is down again today
so I escape by wondering if love
begins like a block of marble
in need of fair subtraction
or like a blank canvas
to which I must add
Maybe neither but I'm
attracted to the musky perfume
of mystery so when I get drawn
through a doorway with the word
LOVE carved into its lintel
I pay attention to the dew
and wait for the first bird to deliver
its call like a cactus flower
to the blank page
Butterflies turn
into orphans of sleep
beneath a bristle of stars
or into century plants so slow
you think they will fizzle
It might take a budding oak
to sort this out
I'll head south for the winter
in search of new solar energy
and wait for that grave digger
to bury my mind-trips and memories
I thought of plotting this
as a graph with a time abscissa
and love ordinate but it might
look too much like the market
If only I could bundle my losses
into derivatives and retire
to 1515 Almond Beach Drive
Cayman Islands I would

Missing

Somewhere
on a sidewalk
in the wet cement
of our youth
two sets of initials
still co-exist
inside a heart
now hardened
by time
yet go on emitting
rhythmic beats
like the black box
from a missing
airplane

Mask of Bravado

Think of it as a strongbox
structured
to guard treasures—
decorated
as though a treasure itself
jeweled surfaces
glinting in the sun
its contents
a mass of discontent
and fear   fear
that someone
might come to know
its contents

In Sleep

We stride
      our steed
            each knight
across the wide berth of heaven
striking sparks on paved firmament
lapping through the milky way
           then in retro
      come back
to Earth

Flip Switch Pantoum

Every time I flicker on
you flicker off or just go dim
whether or not the shades are drawn
making me think you're thinking of him

you flicker off or just go dim
beneath the sheets you refuse to stir
making me think you're thinking of him
so I flip my switch and think of her

beneath the sheets you refuse to stir
like a naked statue that cannot move
so I flip my switch and think of her
it helps me get back in the groove

like a naked statue that cannot move
whether or not the shades are drawn
it helps me get back in the groove
every time I flicker on

At The Peace Café

I love the feeling of *foreign*
of being dunked in the unfamiliar
pastel stuccos and cobbled streets
crooked windows and checkerboard
speech all adding up to anonymity

And so I understand why the odd-
looking couple in dark lederhosen
and dirndl with their feather-tipped
hats approaching the outdoor café
where I'm nursing my cappuccino

remark in awe at the quaintness
of the rusty wrought-iron railing
made out of welded-together
peace symbols that surrounds
the hand-hewn wooden tables

where customers tie their dogs
next to a carved bird-scaring owl
as a pink panel truck delivers
morning bananas and a boy pushes
a dolly stacked with donut boxes

It's much the same as getting over
a jilted love affair   an after-shower
cleansing   but from the inside out
as though some sort of forgiveness
has been miraculously achieved

without the usual humility or prayer
I glance up from my newspaper
in time to see her pick up a napkin
dab powdered sugar from his goatee
two lovers immersed in a foreign land

A Good Book

As I look out from its pages
the world seems backwards

hunger reduced to a beckoning
of the corner gelato shop

plot locks the door with a simple turn
of its deadbolt

love can bloom in here like marigolds
luring frenzied honey bees

as can the vines of anarchy
the ragged weeds of greed and lust

yet freedom cannot be found
by lurking behind the lace curtain

and so I mingle with boisterous words
meditate on the magic of their images

drink coffee with their dénouements
then extricate myself to view the world

through a wider window lest I remain
that mere shadow in a cowslip meadow

where mosquitoes are but flying bits
of somebody else's blood

Starlet's Pantoum Companion

A thinking woman never sleeps with monsters
unless perhaps her thoughts are misconstrued
like the starlet who was sure she'd win an Oscar
by playing parts where she is mostly nude

Unless perhaps her thoughts are misconstrued
like deadly sins served on a silver saucer
by playing parts where she is mostly nude
while knowing there are better things to offer

Like deadly sins served on a silver saucer
marring beauty   making her look crude
while knowing there are better things to offer
for well-endowed does not mean well-imbued

Marring beauty   making her look crude
it mainly frustrates those who want to sponsor
for well-endowed does not mean well-imbued
these are guidelines she'll be called to answer

It mainly frustrates those who want to sponsor
like the starlet who was sure she'd win an Oscar
these are guidelines she'll be called to answer
a thinking woman never sleeps with monsters

Painted Birds of the Tang Dynasty

I live in this city where the department of lost
and found dreams is filled with stuff
that belongs to somebody else
Here night creeps in like a fog   haloing
streetlights   turns narrow canyon floors
into rivers of yellow fish that swim
back and forth in ever-congesting schools

The dingy bar far below my tenth floor loft
ramps up decibels of too many beers arguing
over traded clicks of billiard balls
I spend too much of life in this lonely space
squeezed between my *ifs* and *whens*
sky-scrapers robbing the healing blue of sky
encasing me like the history of a forest
concealed within its tree rings

I wonder if there are words to win over
my feelings so I can survive like an uncaught
rainbow trout arching the wide horizon
after a showy Idaho thunderstorm
My daily walks are past outdated freight yards
and glassed-in mannequins   I long
for the smell of sweet cedar boughs
stacked crates of fruit waiting in an orchard

A magic lamp from a pawn shop down the street
though dented and tarnished keeps hinting
it will aid and abet me in leaping this sky-line
At least a gentle rubbing always brings me hope
I open my eyes and focus on the splash of red
poppies erupting from a hand-painted Chinese
vase delivered from the florist this morning
its ancient symbols of freedom   underscoring

birds in flight   The very sight of it evokes
sleek black feathers—makes a blackbird
of me—another way of looking
                        at the wings I will need
                                to escape this city

The Breath of Life

Huddled in a foxhole
feeling the clay
of mortality

Inhaling   exhaling
thinking of Julie
back home

how she had plucked
wild cherries
for him to savor

Nightlife

Molly sits musing at a small table
near the one un-curtained window
in her ninth-floor room at The Abbey

a hotel that has earned its reputation
as the best one-step-up-from-homeless
dive in this so-called city of bent dreams

She stares at the one Marlboro stub
still smoldering in a cut-glass ashtray
ice chips melting to nothing on her tongue

the smoke encircles her view of the Empire
Club marquee across the way where she once
kicked high her now varicose-veined legs

Sleep has become her ex-lover
living somewhere around the Mediterranean
behind arched doors of a cathedral

She curses the loud ticking of the clock
her lungs stealing just enough air
for each goddamn to be pushed out

If one of the well-to-do gentleman waiting
for a taxi tickles her fancy she flashes
a smile and waves and if he starts counting

to nine on his fingers as he jay-walks
Molly rushes to the cracked wall-mirror
with her lipstick and grabs her pink boa

but most of the time no one notices her
signal and she becomes that still-folded
napkin on the table after the club has closed

watching the skyline slowly roll toward
another rude awakening in morning light
paint flakes accumulating on the window sill

Spiraling Toward Anonymity

Mornings I look into the mirror and say
          to myself   *I miss you*

Evenings I sit on a bar stool no longer
          feeling absent

Life goes on singing and I am just one
          of its many songs

I avoid thinking of dark parts of my past
          by tucking them

into manila envelopes hoping 30 years
          will pass before I remember

Time ticks like the swishing of the bar mop
          at closing

sometimes filling me with unspeakable
          sadness or sorrow

The world keeps asking who I am and I say
          to myself   *I wish I knew*

Inner City

let us dive into the depths
of this city to see
what happens to us

flop in some torn-towel hotel
drink in sirens by night
jackhammers by day

stalk sooty sidewalks
sniff the blasts of diesel busses
steam from sidewalk grates

needle through tattoo parlors
bling-marts decked out
in high-security garb

snicker at tuxedos and furs
chauffeured in from the suburbs
to jockey beneath lighted marquees

frequent open-door barrooms
lit up by juke boxes in the back
stench of beer and vomit

and resolve to conquer this city
by total surrender
to some inner madness

then babble insanities to passersby
unaware that what's happened to us
has been happening for centuries

Across From Molly's Diner

He stands on the sidewalk in a city
where they don't speak his language

leans against graffiti-clad bricks
on the windowless side of City Drugs

He's already had his morning coffee
across the street in Molly's Diner

paid for his fried eggs and toast with
loose change from yesterday's handouts

But cute little kind-hearted Molly
always says *The coffee's on me   Luv*

He likes the sound of the word   *Luv*
how Molly punctuates it with pursed lips

his secret desire to someday marry her
is embossed across a collage of fantasies

that from time to time replace each other
to drown out the white noise of the city

At 2 a.m. he watches her close up shop
from his cardboard box across the street

wonders what she'll be going home to
as street cleaners drone in the distance

Maybe I'll do sunny side up tomorrow
he thinks as the night folds in around him

He'll be standing here again tomorrow
like someone who has missed his bus

Global Warming

Man-made or cyclical
who knows but the possibility
either is true sends chills
up my duty-bound spine

Imagine hunger
tethered to a tent stake
next to an empty barn's
lengthy shadow

Summer heat
the color of glowing
filaments of hot tungsten
spiraling skyward

Otherwise ordinary days
coming unstitched
as dragonflies skirt la playa
in search of pond water

A discarded riding boot
caught on barbed wire
provides a final-resting place
for skinny pigeons

I wonder if my solar panels
will save the icecaps
as sunlight tightens its noose
around the neck of existence

Breakup on the Dance Floor

—after Hotel Room   Patterns of Light by Kate Gale

I remember how you tried to out-drink me
sang that song from one Midwest dancehall
to **another** about how happy you were to know
your place in life   Yes you were beautiful
in a way I've almost forgotten and you said
you were in my life to make a difference
And you sketched pictures on café napkins
always a yellow daisy pushing up through
a jagged crack as though a single flower might
overcome   And that time you ran home
to your mother in Chicago   When you got back
you said   Honey I slept with a homeless guy
over Christmas   had to find out what it's like
to bring a soul back to life in a cardboard box
I remember light bouncing off the dance floor
and how it pierced my eyes   then darkened
I swallowed unable to utter a word like a spineless
lizard   As I was leaving   I threw down the last
napkin flower   You just stared as you sat there
rocking   Don't leave me you said   but you looked
empty   You were vanishing right there between
me and the door   voice barely audible   fading
like a car radio entering an underpass   I walked out
into clean rain   Last I heard you were tending bar
down in Peoria   taking life one shot glass at a time

My First Counseling Session

My shrink tells me
to peel the onion
even if it makes me cry

I need to slough off
layers of denial
get to the long forgotten
root causes

So I begin to peel
and there under the first layer
is Andrea
in her blood red mini-skirt
black patent leather spikes

I want her back
but I keep on peeling
and find Brenda
stretched out
on a beach towel
in her striped bikini
bottom with no top
face down   gorgeous
tan shoulder blades
our *ete* on the French Riviera

I want her back
oh how I want her back
but next comes Cynthia
candles all a-flicker
hot Jacuzzi whipping up steam

O I could go on and on
all the way to the end

of the alphabet
but when I reach Ophelia
I melt
raving and ravenous

So I blend it all
in a Teflon skillet
over medium heat
with extra virgin
olive oil and oregano

Sauté the savory delight
until each layer has clarity
edged in golden brown
then with a crust of bread
and a glass of Chardonnay
I pronounce myself cured
and desert the shrink

Fox Hunt

—*We're on the side of the animal
that's being chased*—Norman Jewison

It's a cold November morning in the middle
of another fox hunt   my father in his red
and black checked jacket   pant legs loosely
stuffed pirate-style into a pair of turned-down
hip boots   loaded double-barreled shotgun
slung over his right shoulder   I'm the one
in the surplus pea coat from Salvation Army
with my don't-shoot-me-red stocking cap
pulled down over my ears   feeling sorry
for the fox yet banging on one of my mother's
saucepans with her favorite serving spoon

The noise is hard to bear as the clanging echoes
through snow-clad fields and drifted fencerows
for there are dozens of slightly-skewed versions
of me and my father closing in on the culprit's
suspected den   Late last night down at Blazing's
Tavern the men had decided that this harasser
of Old Man Frick's chickens must die

I smell the hint of alcohol chilling in the crisp
morning air and can almost hear a warning bell
I cringe at the sight of a sleek gray tail   Years
will pass before I come to know how a few beers
can shut out the deafening volley   the bleeding
the glee in a father's voice as he shouts *Tally Ho*

Another Night at Bully's

Into the crystal ball
of a half-empty stemmed goblet
I gaze   transfixed—
a partially-cut piece of lathe-work
begging to be finished

I delay the deal that needs
to be dealt with
blame it on inertia that must
first be overcome   Is it fear
of what's ahead or just a simple

wish not to disturb that perfectly
machined beauty of the present
Life is a stage upon which I play
the nine lives of a Cheshire cat
in seven separate acts

each an unfinished glass
of wine wanting to be consumed—
rough-cut, half-lathed stock
still firmly gripped in the vise
The clock on the half-plastered wall

must feel it—that endless unwinding
of main spring   Life
goes on with or without us
but when the crystal ball begins to blur
it's time to stop—after just one more

Anonymity

It had been a particularly awkward afternoon
and I of course was looking for a way to opt out

The unsteady sidewalk seemed to move in odd ways
and the storefront reflections bent me out of shape

I ducked into a little hole called Twelfth Street Bar
hoping that somehow I'd become totally anonymous

The Tudor walls with mahogany trim gave it class
but not enough to douse the smell of yesterday's beer

You were seated on a barstool about halfway down
tight short skirt   crossed legs   red leather heels

I took the adjacent stool and you laughed when I said
that my goal-of-the-day was complete anonymity

We downed double shots of bourbon to make it happen
then seconds   and that's when things became blurry

I ran into you again years later in a 12-Step meeting
You said   *Looks like you finally achieved your goal*

Quiet Realm

yawning face of yellow
        moon
no lyrics   no tune

outward ripples from cattail
        stalk
no reason   to talk

leaf smoke drifting from autumn
        fire
stringless   lyre

listening to Spirit in the quiet
        realm
sensing   its helm

bubbles bowing to vanishing
        touch
our life   is such

the stones for a moment
        sigh
no tears   to cry

On the Wings of Meditation

After long winter rains on a little hilltop over-
looking the sea beneath an inverted singing-bowl

sky   cross-legged   I meld into a host
of birdsong emanating from sacred pines

I swoop from lobe to lobe in meditation
easing through a complex of labyrinth corridors

Sometimes I become a pelican flying home
beak pouch bulging with savory treasures

Other times a proud stork atop a chimney flue
taking credit for increases in the population

Today I am standing on one leg in frothy surf
a pink-feathered flamingo surveying possibilities

Suddenly we are two   sleek coral necks entwined
glowing along the ocean front   pink neon of dusk

Conversations with Solitude

Go sit near that hollow of trees beyond the field-line
uncover the questions waiting in the shadow of a great rock
mull them over but do not worry about the answers
they will be fed to you like thread from an unwinding spool

Quench your thirst   fill your lungs with expanding air
taste the foreign language of Indian Summer
let the blemish on each falling leaf cradle your thoughts
blurring the shapes of trees in a smudge of smoke

Our gardens within are patches of pure grace
humanity is the sole author of all flotsam and jetsam
there is a fool in every   court and often it is the king
we thrive and reproduce on borrowed dust   borrowed time

That house you thought empty might be peopled with solitude
an important yet often neglected segment of the populace
night and day lead such different lives   touching
only twice in 24 hours   once at dusk   once at dawn

So if the briar patch tugs at your sweater   stay a bit longer
commune with the mystery hidden inside each stone   each leaf
life is the slow opening of an inner eye   our ear to its silence
overhead two crows loop in spirals across a cloudless sky

Deep in Swami's Garden

I fondle two smooth stones
one in each hand
as I sit in meditation

focusing on time's threshold
the way Da Vinci's
Vitruvian Man straddles space

The breathing of the waves
is like an inward and outward
flow of prayer

At high tide the beach
is swallowed   at low tide
littered with ornaments of death

I wonder about death   Is it soft
like feathers or like this fallen leaf
disconnected and leathery

I pry open my soul   hoping
for God   but the shadow
of my father fills the garden

It's as though
I've been chained to a wall
deep inside Plato's cave

unable to overcome the mysteries
of this world   the strange
musings of a meditative mind

Life comes and goes in cycles
like endless waves   so maybe
death is simply the end of a cycle

I'd like to get my father's opinion
but I know his shadow
won't supply the answer

Somewhere nearby a finch begins
a new song   clear and clean
as the fingerprints of rain

Birds too must have souls   surely
God would not be so frugal
as to deny any creature that

By now the stones are heavier
they've absorbed my concerns and so
I give them to gravity's pull

Sometimes it's Hard to Speak Up

If only the Earth could speak for me
not in mere images or metaphors
for who can translate the meaning
of a grove of giant Redwoods
or a volcano spewing ash and lava

And think of the timid primrose
peeking through a crack
in the desert floor
somehow knowing that once broken
silence loses its innocence

Someone once tried to convince me
that sneezes and orgasms
are near-death experiences since they
temporarily block out the world
and stifle coherent speech

From my back window I watch
volunteers uprooting non-native vegetation
for disposal and am reminded of how
political correctness urges certain words
to live and die in my throat

So it is with gratitude that I kneel in prayer
on this magic carpet knowing I need the world
more than it needs me as I keep trying
to fool myself and others until poetry
that gateway to Heaven   emancipates

Pantoum to Morning Meditation

As I sit in meditation while the world goes fleeting by
with faith in firmness of solid ground beneath my humble feet
I seek images serene like grassy meadows   woods or sky
when fears or worries come my way   I quickly press delete

With faith in firmness of solid ground beneath my humble feet
I focus on celestial bodies   planets   moons and stars
when fears or worries come my way   I quickly press delete
to aid in my escape from self-constructed prison bars

I focus on celestial bodies   planets   moons and stars
tipping my hat to mighty Orion while strolling the Milky Way
to aid in my escape from self-constructed prison bars
imagination's plan for me to survive another day

Tipping my hat to mighty Orion while strolling the Milky Way
my giant stride keeps up the pace   each step must span a mile
imagination's plan for me to survive another day
make my peace with Mother Earth and greet *you* with a smile

My giant stride keeps up the pace   each step must span a mile
I seek images serene like grassy meadows   woods or sky
make my peace with Mother Earth and greet *you* with a smile
as I sit in meditation while the world goes fleeting by

Renewal

—after The Journey
by David Whyte

Above the Torrey Pine-covered hill
a single hawk arcs into
the rays of morning

like an accomplished calligrapher
inscribing downward spirals
on a translucent canopy

as though to say his message
requires the lofty medium
of sky-writing

in order to reach down
and touch words
already circulating within you

We often look toward
the skies or beyond
to magnify the

miniscule seeds of freedom
longing to burst forth
from our own being

And there are times
when a friend will come to carry
away the ashes

of a spent campfire
and help you pull up stakes
with the understanding

this is not the end
You are ready to move on

The Messiah

During the peaceful reign of Caesar Augustus
The Roman Empire had grown to encompass
the landmasses bordering the Mediterranean Sea

The deserts surrounding Jerusalem were harsh
and long trips were marred by the possibility
that one of the travelers might die along the way

It was a custom of that time to bury the dead
near their ancestral homes so travelers had to be
prepared to transport bodies over long distances

And yet the faithful came in droves to Jerusalem
by caravan   by foot   by donkey   to pay
homage and make sacrifice to their one great God

Men in the caravans wound long strips of gauze
around their waists so in the event of a death
it could be used to swaddle and preserve the body

Overnight Inns along the way provided shelters
for animals they brought along to be sacrificed
on the stone altar of The Temple in Jerusalem

So when a called census required Joseph and Mary
who was great with child to travel from Nazareth
to Bethlehem Joseph wound his waist in swaddling

The Inn was filled so they stayed with the animals
where Mary gave birth to Jesus and wrapped Him
in Joseph's swaddling and laid him in a manger

Shepherds arrive to find Jesus in a sacrificial lamb's
feeding trough and as angels had said   wrapped
in swaddling cloth so they know He *is* The Messiah

Where There is Dark
There is Also Light

We are flawed
yet masterful inventions
blinded by life's little pleasures and pains
forced to laugh and cry out of the same two eyes

We use each other
to heal unwarranted sufferings
the way a hand on a child's bruised head
shows us how misery is distracted by company

We bow to the sound
of applause   the clamors of war
the golden rule a peculiar imbedded tune
and sometimes on summer nights we sleep in the nude

A turbulent water flows
beneath our narrow bridges and nothing
no thing   not even one thing is stationary
especially that hitch-hiker love   dim lamp in hand

We are sentenced
to find order amidst the tempest
but words can be either life-rafts or flotsam
hang like a heavy mist long after the ship goes down

The dead don't give
a damn whether we cry or not
they become our burdens   heavier than sacks
of potatoes ignoring busy streets and flowers and you & me

We gather bundles
of firewood in late morning
as a light snow turns the world into graveyard
the way death likes to copy every picture ever drawn by life

The diameter of the bomb
is always small compared to its concentric
circles of death and dismemberment and sometimes
even ordinary love devours all of its surrounding points of view

So as you cycle
between life's two handfuls of dust
wriggle out from under the shadow of the rock
run free in the meadows   you'll find light blooming there

The Source

There is an underbelly
to the soul
that rules its back alleys

feeds on stones
beneath a dim lamp
which burns

both day and night
with a persistently licking
dark gray flame

which we must learn
to reduce to shadows
by using a brighter light

fueled by power
not from within
but of our Creator

The Golden Apple

We are all but recent leaves on the same
old tree of life—Albert Szent-Györgyi

Deep inside the pulp of apple
packed in a suitcase of harvested fruit
eternal flame is safe forever

for even when the flesh is eaten
seeds of hope remain within its core
prepared for reproduction

while outside its regal fragile skin
burly old fruit trees grow gnarly
and perish in mist and rain

Reflections on Water

When into the willowed creek
of our own shallow understanding
we watchfully wade
reflecting on the morning sun
breath   heartbeat   clouds
rotation of planets   the water
calm as an empty spoon
and like love   filling every void
we drink of each other
quenching our thirsty souls
that we may rise out of darkness
like two seedling sprouts
poking empty heads up
through fertile soil   not forgetting
that we are but ripples
moving out from splashes
of love   so toss in a few coins
let the fountains play

Pantoum Prayer

Invest me in this day of yours   Oh Lord
Your purity sweeps through me like a breeze
send loaves and fishes to the hungry horde
and this I humbly plead from bended knees

Your purity sweeps through me like a breeze
It's a harmony that forms the perfect chord
and this I humbly plead from bended knees
Your grace will add to what I can't afford

It's harmony that forms the perfect chord
the opening of that one great eye that sees
Your grace will add to what I can't afford
When doors are locked You offer up the keys

The opening of that one great eye that sees
a plowshare rated higher than the sword
When doors are locked You offer up the keys
provide an ark that all who will can board

A plowshare rated higher than the sword
gives us the peace of flowers   sky and trees
provides an ark that all who will can board
each of Your days is here for us to seize

I pray that You will hear my humble pleas
send loaves and fishes to the hungry horde
make peace abound   our enemies appease
Invest me in this day of yours   Oh Lord

My Philosophy

I suppose the separation
of light and dark started it all
the way a single brush stroke
might save a lifeless painting
It seems like shadows might
give us a clue   I'm still trying
to piece things together   It's like
finding mates in a box of old shoes

The stoic sky ignores our petty
desires   which are endless tangles
anyway   We are pinned to the bulletin
board of life   Bridges as well as rooftop
gardens were constructed specifically
for lovers   Everything we see is light
reflected off darker objects   flame's
fiery knots   tying then untying

Coal would be counted as a jewel
if it didn't burn   Cherry blossoms scatter
at the first sight of rain   Unpainted boats
float on the waters of our childhood
Look deeper into the unimportant rustlings
of leaves   Birth is but death in reverse
and you and I are living proof of that

My Life as a Chain Unwinding
Through a Cinquain Labyrinth
—after "The Layers"
by Stanley Kunitz

I've lived
through many lives
which change from age to age
unfurling from a central core
called self

I peer
through a rear-view
mirror called memory
to gather courage for dealing
with life

I watch
milestones dwindle
from abandoned campsites
still attended to by caring
angels

I've made
myself a tribe
of scattered affections
hoping my heart will respond to
each loss

The wind
raises the dust
of my many past friends
yet the road ahead is precious
to me

One dark
night while roaming
the wreckage I was told

to savor the layers not the
litter

And though
I find it hard
to decipher those words
I sense they mean that changes lie
ahead

Beyond Comprehension

The door slams shut and just like that
it's over   signaling either an end

or a beginning depending on which side
of the door fate has planted your feet

Behind it afternoon light scales down
like accordion pleats at the end of a polka

but in front of it morning light scales up
spreads open like a Japanese fan

and it all happens at the speed of light
unwilling to fit into human scale

Lifesong

A single moment thinner than a razor blade
yet wide as the years I've spent on earth
can bring joy or sorrow up from the cellar

lift and fall like a great white blanket of fog
hovering between valley and mountain brow
clearing then clouding the quaking aspens

I skim along the tops of lined-up dominos
from fallen to falling and just in the nick of time
having no clue as to when the string will end

It's been a long lazy summer of flip-flops
tank-tops and backward baseball hats but now
the pigeons are putting on coats of city soot

I can't waste nor throw away anything
for nothing belongs to me in the first place
I am here simply to stir things around

Love abounds   helps me shape things
into place   though at times invisible
no sparks until blade touches grindstone

I learned to carry the tunes that carry me
to dance with the moon till it no longer shines
and when lyrics are garbled to digest the melody

Heads or Tails

I flip the coin of grief
it comes up tails
I cry

I flip again
it comes up heads
once more I cry

Unfair   I say
and yet I go on flipping
till it drops

rolls under
my bed or armoire
out of sight

where it will linger
entertaining tarnish
and gathering dust

or else I spend it
trade it in for joy
summoned up

by some unconscious
recollection of tossing
coins in a fountain

as shadows of pigeons
busy themselves
like angels

Fishing on Sylvan Lake

Lazy cane poles
    angle skyward
        willing to wait hours
for a single unsuspecting fish
    to take its bait

A mucky smell
    of dead fish
        roused by the warm sun
permeates partly-shaded water
    between willow branches

weeping trees that dance
    upside down
        in green water
as a sunfish splashes the surface
    to brandish its rainbow scales

A baby frog
    learns to jump
        from a lily pad
as bullfrogs full of brave adventure
    croak from the marshy shore

Dragon-flies hover
    over the white spires
        of tiny red-ball bobbers
little churches floating aloof
    responding to each jerk of the pole

sending out concentric ripples
    of communication
        to the rest of the world
that fishing here on Sylvan Lake
    is more than just catching a fish

Game On

think falling out of your mother's womb
        then crawling across open country under fire
                until you drop into your grave
think it's all downhill from wet-naked and hungry
        think sunshine   freedom   little flower
                hyphen between matter and spirit
think dancing at an un-hoped for party
        think wishbone, backbone, funny-bone
                letting go and holding on
think time to reexamine
        if knees aren't green
                by the end of the day
think 'I'm with ya kid' as you take it by the lapel
        think cup filled with laughter
                superb cast with unmanageable plot
think multiple choice with a final
        tough essay question
                dinner with dessert served first
think ten-speed bicycle with most of the gears un-used
        think measured out with coffee spoons
                licking honey off a thorn
think tearing up one rough draft after another
        think fill what's empty and empty what's full
                occupy   occupy   occupy
think book of questions with no answers in the back
        think concrete trampoline or frayed bungee cord
                think   then think again

Galileo

Not much has changed since Galileo
          though subways sparkle
                    in Singapore
and we've moved from implements
          to appliances
                    to devices
Rain still pelts the broken bird feeders
          and couples still make out
                    beneath lilac bushes
Life goes on being that misbehaving child
          turning itself inside out
                    like an odd sock
No ceilings to inhibit rebellious minds
          and wild horses go mostly
                    untamed
Galileo's moon-track showed mountains
          and valleys so maybe Earth is
                    a heavenly body as well
after all its angels spend lives on lovers
          and friends while sparrows
                    mock them in leafless trees
I once had a cat named Galileo
          who spent days staring first at one
                    sparrow   then another

Apologia

It may not take a genius to design
        a simple machine but I can't see
                how one might simply evolve

just as oceans are not here
        by circumstance and a simple dance
                never brings rain

so from behind the trimmed hedges
        of righteousness as I prop up
                my fallen beams of self esteem

I applaud the Great Inventor's
        will for all that has passed
                my way and passes still

But oh how I love to nourish
        those lies that are willing to sit
                quietly in my mind and grow

until they can pace back and forth
        in that cage where excuses to live it up
                and endurance mingle

My refuse pile of second chances
        is filled with ramshackle trade-ins
                of failed romances

and the dead-letter office of mixed metaphors
        has rejected my   *Eat drink and be merry*
                for tomorrow never comes

which may be true even as the dark shoes
        of death are being cobbled
                to fit pre-measured feet

Awakening
—after Emergence by Joy Harjo

Lit by a thousand distant ancestral campfires
the July night air scintillates with moisture
and coats the grass with the dew of desire
The dogs are turned on by the wafting scent
of the willingness in other dogs to go wild

I dangle dangerously in this deep crevice
created by a recently ripped open heart
my body flailing against willpower's walls
It's unraveling and the whole world knows
even the wild nasturtiums breaking out

in their fiery oranges and nightshade purples
So too the giver of grace who plays Pied
Piper with his merry band of pranksters
know-it-all hearts that go on pumping blood
There was a time when we all shared

this one big piece of real estate as a globe
without fences and we called it our garden
and we worked together to enhance its beauty
Nothing like the way it has recently erupted
entering the marrow of my bones as I bounce

off the walls of my little box to the commercial
beat of TV ads from the little box next door
I begin to think that maybe I do need Viagra
or that I should get my windshield repaired
when I have no problem getting an erection

and my Mercedes is new and without flaw
My mind shrinks when I get fed such drivel
I need to find refuge in the realm of the creator
of my daily bread my occasional dose of love
and figure out how to escape these jaws of desire

maybe by depriving myself of all sustenance
until I can clamber up the walls of this crevice
leaving the luggage of grief behind as I loosen
the reins of the rising sun from the hands of Helios
and ride his gilded chariot into a new and better day

American Sky

The sky's open to all   even you who ripped
       a gap in the picket fence of my psyche
            that will go un-mended

Our accordion of permissiveness
       pays little attention to race hustlers
            ethnic and gender busters

Consider the bumble bee who knows
       nothing of the laws of aerodynamics
            yet flies anyway

On tangled freeway interchanges
       the ambulance of art always arrives
            with its lights and sirens

and the moon   round like a pea
       with its *so-what* camouflaged smile
            is wanting to be planted somewhere

Alchemy

discard
your diary
with its daily
drudgery
and come
with me
to that place
in the sun
whether
in the gloved
hands
of winter
or the bare
feet
of summer
where beauty
is visible
to all
who love
turning fears
and anxieties
into golden
coins
for eternal
spending

Change

I give change the attention a painter
gives her canvas as she develops
the agitation just above the break
of a wave   or whitewashes in
the twilight glow of a waning moon
as background for her ring-billed gull

All of life's cycles can be seen
as bouquets meant to be passed along
to the next season waiting patiently
Witness the deep green of Summer
on its way out handing to the forest
a chameleon's palette of Autumn colors

I drift in a sea of Queen Anne's Lace
watching two-way traffic from meadow
flower to beehive's golden cells
completely immersed in the paradise
of participation and the buzz that all things
embedded in time are meant to change

We are Born to Die

Some say life is the dash between dates inscribed on a tombstone
or a parenthetical phrase and we can't see beyond either end

Each new day we punch our way out of yesterday's paper bag
sometimes wanting to sink with the dregs to the bottom of the cup

I look back at my childhood as just another long lost friend
but when I think of death I think of losing all my friends

Clouds are born daily   do their work   then die in the same sky
as the sun scribbles a postscript before disappearing again

We try to liberate ourselves by living in metaphor or simile
as the dead fall around us like rain   snow   like volcanic ash

When summer dies she makes her grand exit in a painted hearse
leaving behind entire hillsides of unwanted ragweed and thistle

Then the husks and weed-seeds of dying autumn turn brittle
precursors of treacherous winter with his merciless snowplow

We hang on to life like frantic wasps clinging to shriveled peaches
until we lose those invisible gears and levers that kept us moving

Death's roving eye can whip up a myth-a-minute   then devour it
like rumors in a town with one main street and a host of back alleys

And not until we accept ourselves as quarry strapped to Death's steed
does the earth seem earthier   stones stonier   stars starrier indeed

Unbridled

The stallion I encountered yesterday
    bucking through wild meadow grass
        insisted he was pure imagination

His demeanor was one of boldness
    but his deep almost-human voice
        convinced me he was legit

My owner decided to ditch the bridle
    because it damped my creativity
        told me to think unicorn

And from what I know about unicorns
    it's going to take the sight and scent
        of a spirited mare to tame me

Even imagining her smooth dappled coat
    and dark eyes triggers an untangling
        in my unkempt mane

As I await her manifestation I bide my time
    trampling wild daisies
        and polishing my twisted horn

Leaving it up to the motive power
    of pure imagination to propel us both
        into the Happy-Ever-After

Early Harvest

Love can grow faster than corn
—the harvest ears of August
were but kernels in the fertile soil
of spring—but so can cancer

Brief encounters with radiation
longer ones with chemotherapy
hurrying life's declension
my heart in some waiting room

A mirror breathes   tries to smile
pink lap robes and teddy bears
headscarves and baseball caps

Hope is based on what's left
but at the end   couldn't it be
confetti   rather than ashes

Saturday: Baking Day

Though days sift through your fingers
like sprinkled flour on the pastry board

a fresh-baked loaf of heartache is too hot
to lay even a finger on as you remember

your mitted mother hurrying from oven
to that over-used blackened wire rack

that would cradle her measure of daily life
until properly cooled for the cutting board

So much of memory resides outside of us
rises up through yeasty warmth of dough

Nothing packages neatly into the bundle
of death   especially fresh-baked bread

which can bring a breath out of the grave
like afternoon light crossing the kitchen

Gone to Seed

Lying with you in tall grass
among dandelions
beneath bold summer's sky
its morphing clouds
tigress turning into heart
then breasts   whale changing
into a phallus
yellow of dandelion
reflecting from curves
and crevices of our bodies
fusing us into each other
forming a single nebula
as dandelions dance
in the breeze

Autumn now and you
no longer here   I wade
that same tall grass
taller now   turning brown
dandelions gone to seed
long stems still standing
each a multitude
of tiny parachutes
ethereal memories
ready to punctuate
the passing breeze
ghosts of last summer

For Bernie

Suddenly it's one o'clock on Monday
and I want to put him back in the chair
where he emptied his heart and mind
onto the wood-grained library table
in the presence of poets and friends

He had a chuckle that changed a bit
when anyone mentioned the word God
even wanted it spelled in lower case
He viewed the contest between intellect
and faith as just another zero-sum game

I remember how he cackled out loud
at the errant monk in one of my poems
To him it was an oxymoron but I think
it struck a bell for it rang true to his belief
that good and bad are like East and West

So here's to the man once wrapped in dark
now slowly and steadily being un-wrapped
free to dream in one of God's mansions
May his brilliance be added to the heavens
the candle-power of his essence to the stars

How Grief Ends and When

Our worlds of joy and sorrow flowed like the oceans' tides
and we drew our lines between them in the shifting sand

Pier pilings pointed to possibilities beyond the far horizon
as seagulls fluttered their acceptance of God-given gifts

You were the lighthouse lamp that led me safely to solitude
for my soul was caught in the tangles of your hair

The musical measures of your heartbeat were signs of hope
like the opening hands of leaves that welcomed Spring

Your beauty rose out of various imbalances of perfection
the way fog hides the sun yet makes the world a-drip with dew

We are all refugees in time   greeting   collecting and dropping
memorabilia along the way between hellos and goodbyes

And like the dark and dirty lowdown blues we listened to
one storm rarely passes without another on its way

Although your life was dazzling and brief like that of a desert rose
you were an angel who had earned your wings

And wouldn't we all like to know how grief ends and when
I'm almost positive the far-off fires of stars know the answer

Late Harvest

Only turnips and a few carrots remain
and frost has caused
the purple chrysanthemums to turn
I'm wearing gloves
an extra heavy wool shirt
as I reach out from my shaky perch
on a ladder against
a high limb of the apple tree
to pick fruit missed at early harvest
What's left of the pyracantha berries
intoxicates a flock of pesky blue jays
The puffy clouds could pass
for cotton balls and only a few
leaves are left on the walnut tree
As I pause to re-set my watch
I think of the earth's willingness
to spin on a tilted axis—
how over in the desert   war continues
to make daily entries in its journal
while clusters of golden dates
hang from palm trees
begging to be picked

And Life Goes On...

Another year   another circumvention
     naked Earth in orbit
         irresistible sun tugging

Ruptured tectonic plates
     react to perpetual motion
         every move predestined

Muscle-flexings of a loving God
     eighty-eight piano keys plus
         death and birth in harmony

Inscriptions on stone tablets
     and promises of mansions
         bribe us into strict obedience

Leafy woods and meadows
     eager for romping
         await our indulgence

Beneath oblivious skies
     symmetry dances with chaos
         energy in motion

Night and day again   and then again
     children follow in our footsteps
         exuberant and unknowing

The Sky is Not the Limit

nor is the sea with its endless
churning
and certainly not the heart
pumping its life-giving blood
and spreading God's love of mankind

In first grade when I opened
a new box of crayons
my eyes and fingers were drawn
to red   yellow and blue
a trinity that creates all color

a reminder of that limitless presence
and power of the Holy Trinity
God the Father
          God the Son
                    God the Holy Spirit

Acknowledgments

Ode to The Pencil, p 287, R. T. Sedgwick; The San Diego Poetry Annual, 2011–12; Anthology, William Harry Harding, Publisher: Terrence Spohn *et. al.*, Regional Editors; Garden Oak Press, 1953 Huffstatler St. ,Suite A, Rainbow, CA 92028; ISBN-13: 978-1466466159 & ISBN-10: 1466466154.

The Night-birds; R. T. Sedgwick; McGee Park Poets 2014 Anthology, p 1; Ed. by Ishmael von Heidrick-Barnes, Pub. by Friends of the Carlsbad City Library, 1775 Dove Lane, Carlsbad, CA 92011.

Ripe with Love; R. T. Sedgwick; McGee Park Poets 2012 Anthology, p 37; Ed. by Shadab Zeest Hashmi and Ishmael von Heidrick-Barnes, Pub. by Friends of the Carlsbad City Library, 1775 Dove Lane, Carlsbad, CA 92011.

Summer's Over, p 100, R. T. Sedgwick; The San Diego Poetry Annual, 2011–12; Anthology, William Harry Harding, Publisher: Terrence Spohn *et. al.*, Regional Editors; Garden Oak Press, 1953 Huffstatler St. ,Suite A, Rainbow, CA 92028; ISBN-13: 978-1466466159 & ISBN-10: 1466466154.

Remembrance; R. T. Sedgwick; McGee Park Poets 2015 Anthology, p 56; Ed. by Ishmael von Heidrick-Barnes, Pub. by *The Friends of the Magee Park Poets*, 1775 Dove Lane, Carlsbad, CA 92011.

Lifesong, p 81, R. T. Sedgwick; The San Diego Poetry Annual, 2013–14; Anthology, William Harry Harding, Publisher: Terrence Spohn *et. al.*, Regional Editors; Garden Oak Press, 1953 Huffstatler St. ,Suite A, Rainbow, CA 92028; ISBN-13: 978-1495356940 & ISBN-10: 1495356949.

Game On, p 114, R. T. Sedgwick; The San Diego Poetry Annual, 2012–13; Anthology, William Harry Harding, Publisher: Terrence Spohn *et. al.*, Regional Editors; Garden Oak Press, 1953 Huffstatler St., Suite A, Rainbow, CA 92028; ISBN-13: 978-1482050950 & ISBN-10: 1482050951.

About the Author

R. T. Sedgwick is a poet living in Del Mar, CA. He has numerous published poems and his work appears in several anthologies. His first full length poetry book titled, "Left Unlatched" with sub-title, 'in hopes that you'll come in', 320 pp., published in 2011 by A Word with You Press, Oceanside, CA, was winner of the San Diego Book Awards prize for best poetry book published in 2011. Other poems and additional information can be found on his website, http://www.rtsedgwickpoems.com.

A Word with You Press

Publishers and Purveyors of Fine Stories in the Digital Age

In addition to being a full-service publishing house founded in 2009, A Word with You Press is a playful, passionate, and prolific consortium of writers connected by our collective love of the written word. We are, as well, devoted readers drawn to the notion that there is nothing more beautiful or powerful than a well-told story.

We realize that great writers and artists don't just happen. They are created by nurturing, mentoring, and by inspiration. We provide this literary triad through our interactive website, www.awordwithyoupress.com.

Visit us here to enter our writing contests and to become part of a broad but highly personal writing community. Improve your skills with what has become a significant, de facto writers' workshop, and approach us with your own publishing dreams and ambitions. We are always looking for new talent. Visit our store to buy from a distinguished list of our books, which include the work of a Pulitzer Prize winner, an award-winning poet, and first-rate literary fiction. Attend our seminars and retreats, and consider joining our growing list of published authors.

A writer is among the lucky few who discovers that art is not a diversion or distraction from everyday life; rather, art is an essential expression of the human spirit.

If you are such a writer, join us on our website, www.awordwithyoupress.com. If you have a project to discuss, we will assess the first thirty pages you send us pro-bono. Send your inquiries to the Editor-in-Chief, Thornton Sully, at thorn@awordwithyoupress.com. Be sure to indicate in the subject line "pro-bono assessment" and send your submission as a word doc attachment.

The Mason Key
Volume One
A John Mason Adventure
by David Folz

A street urchin in England about the time the Colonies declare independence cheats the hangman to begin this historical adventure series. He discovers that his father's death may not have been an accident at all, but part of a broader conspiracy.

The Mason Key II
Aloft and Alow
A John Mason Adventure
by David Folz

The historical saga continues as young Mason becomes a mid-shipman on the very ship on which he was as stow-away at the conclusion of *The Mason Key, Volume One*.

The Mason Key III
The Return
A John Mason Adventure
by David Folz

Mason and Marie fend off pirates en route to her father's plantation. John struggles with the Third Principle, Honor, and the Cruelty of Slavery while making his way back home.

Bounce
by Pulitzer Prize winner Jonathan Freedman

A nutty watermelon man, a spurned she-lawyer, a frustrated carioca journalist and a misanthropic parrot set out to Brazil to change the world.

Raw Man

by Pulitzer-Prize nominee Fred Rivera, winner at
the 2015 International Latino Book Awards

This lightly-novelized Vietnam memoir, now required reading
at major universities, derives its title from the author's epiphany:
"Twenty-seven years after I got on the flight home, I saw that Nam
war was just raw man spelled backwards. I'm pretty raw today."

The Boy with a Torn Hat
by Thornton Sully

Debut novel was a finalist in the 2010 USA
Book Awards for Literary Fiction
"Henry Miller meets Bob Dylan in this coming of age romp played
out in the twisted alleyways and smoky beer halls of Heidelberg.
Sully is a cunning wordsmith and master of bringing music to
art and art to language. Excessive, expressive, lusty, and once in
a blue metaphor—profound. Here is what I mean: 'Some women
are imprisoned like a tongue in a bell—they swing violently but
unnoticed until the moment of contact with the bronze perimeter
of their existence—and thenthe sound they make astonishes us its
power and pain and beauty, and its immediacy' —Wunderbar"
—Jonathan Freedman, Pulitzer Prize winner

A Word with You, Vol. I
The Best from A Word with You Press

An anthology of select winners from the literary con-
tests of *A Word with You Press* from 2009 to 2015

Falling for France

by Nancy Milby

The first in *A Foreign Affair* series finds Annie Shaw having to choose between a successful career and real romance with a French aristocrat, and wanting both.

French Twist

by Nancy Milby

The saga continues as American archeologist Louise Marcel becomes entangled in nasty business on French soil, as she conceals her own hidden agenda.

Finding France

by Nancy Milby

The third in *A Foreign Affair* series finds Gabrielle Walker lamenting a life unraveling when a letter informs her she is the inheritor of a large estate in France. Then it gets complicated!

Finding Home

by Nancy Milby

Etienne, the recurring enigma in the series *A Foreign Affair*, is brutal to his enemies but a gentle giant to those he loves. Can the secret woman in his past enter his life again? Perhaps, but not with complications—some predictable, but some …

Visit our on-line store at www.awordwithyoupress.com.
Most books are available as print editions and ebooks. We
have also a growing selection of gifts for writers, and please
check out our latest contests! We'd love a word from you!

A Word with You Press
Publishers and Purveyors of Fine Stories in the Digital Age
310 East A Street
Suite B
Moscow, Idaho 83843

www.ingramcontent.com/pod-product-compliance
Lightning Source LLC
LaVergne TN
LVHW021503080426
835509LV00018B/2380